5th Grade Word of The

Week 1 Use the dictionary to write the definition and divide the words for each day below into syllables.

○ **MONDAY** WORD: *UNICYCLE*
EXAMPLE:

A unicycle is a vehicle that touches the ground with only one wheel.

u-ni-cy-cle

○ **TUESDAY** WORD: *Acrylic*

○ **WEDNESDAY** WORD: *Adage*

○ **THURSDAY** WORD: *Cirque*

○ **FRIDAY** WORD: *Partridge*

○ **SATURDAY / SUNDAY** WORD: *Plateau*

Write Words In ABC Order

_____

_____

_____

_____

_____

For each word, find one synonym & one antonym. (if none: write word + none)

_____

_____

_____

_____

_____

_____

_____

_____

_____

_____

_____

_____

_____

5th Grade Word of The Day

Use the dictionary to write the definition and divide the words for each day below into syllables.

○ MONDAY **WORD:** *Proverb*

Write Words In ABC Order

○ TUESDAY **WORD:** *Conservation*

○ WEDNESDAY **WORD:** *Rhombus*

For each word, find one synonym & one antonym.

○ THURSDAY **WORD:** *Seizure*

○ FRIDAY **WORD:** *Vertical*

○ SATURDAY / SUNDAY **WORD:** *CONQUEST*

5th Grade Word of The Day

Week 3   Use the dictionary to write the definition
and divide the words for each day
below into syllables.

○ MONDAY   WORD: *Sheriff*

Write Words In ABC Order

_____

_____

_____

○ TUESDAY   WORD: *Sediment*

_____

_____

_____

○ WEDNESDAY   WORD: *Tonsil*

For each word, find one synonym
& one antonym.

_____

○ THURSDAY   WORD: *Tranquil*

_____

_____

_____

_____

○ FRIDAY   WORD: *Tremor*

_____

_____

_____

○ SATURDAY / SUNDAY   WORD: *GALAXY*

_____

_____

_____

5th Grade Word of The Day

Week 4   Use the dictionary to write the definition
and divide the words for each day
below into syllables.

○ MONDAY   WORD: *Villain*

Write Words In ABC Order

○ TUESDAY   WORD: *Voucher*

○ WEDNESDAY   WORD: *Whine*

For each word, find one synonym
& one antonym.

○ THURSDAY   WORD: *Wigwam*

○ FRIDAY   WORD: *Vulture*

○ SATURDAY / SUNDAY   WORD: *AEROSPACE*

5th Grade Word of The Day

Use the dictionary to write the definition and divide the words for each day below into syllables.

○ MONDAY **WORD:** *Woodland*

Write Words In ABC Order

_____

_____

_____

_____

_____

_____

○ TUESDAY **WORD:** *Wrench*

○ WEDNESDAY **WORD:** *Unemployment*

For each word, find one synonym & one antonym.

_____

_____

○ THURSDAY **WORD:** *Tropical*

_____

_____

_____

_____

○ FRIDAY **WORD:** *Trio*

_____

_____

_____

_____

○ SATURDAY / SUNDAY **WORD:** *Tariff*

_____

_____

_____

5th Grade Word of The Day

Use the dictionary to write the definition
and divide the words for each day
below into syllables.

○ MONDAY WORD: *Symmetry*

Write Words In ABC Order

○ TUESDAY WORD: *Stencil*

○ WEDNESDAY WORD: *Stampede*

For each word, find one synonym
& one antonym.

○ THURSDAY WORD: *Scarlet*

○ FRIDAY WORD: *Rupture*

○ SATURDAY / SUNDAY WORD: *APPROXIMATE*

5th Grade Word of The Day

Use the dictionary to write the definition and divide the words for each day below into syllables.

○ MONDAY   WORD: *Resist*

Write Words In ABC Order

_____

_____

_____

_____

_____

_____

○ TUESDAY WORD: *Ration*

○ WEDNESDAY   WORD: *Prime*

For each word, find one synonym & one antonym.

_____

_____

_____

_____

○ THURSDAY   WORD: *Pueblo*

_____

_____

_____

_____

○ FRIDAY   WORD: *Porridge*

_____

_____

_____

_____

○ SATURDAY / SUNDAY   WORD: *ACCOMPANY*

_____

_____

_____

5th Grade Word of The Day

Use the dictionary to write the definition
and divide the words for each day
below into syllables.

○ MONDAY WORD: *Perpendicular*

Write Words In ABC Order

○ TUESDAY WORD: *Perch*

○ WEDNESDAY WORD: *Parentheses*

For each word, find one synonym
& one antonym.

○ THURSDAY WORD: *Parallel*

○ FRIDAY WORD: *Oxen*

○ SATURDAY / SUNDAY WORD: *INDICATE*

5th Grade Word of The Day

Use the dictionary to write the definition
and divide the words for each day
below into syllables.

○ MONDAY **WORD:** *Orphan*

Write Words In ABC Order

○ TUESDAY **WORD:** *Oval*

○ WEDNESDAY **WORD:** *Parsley*

For each word, find one synonym
& one antonym.

○ THURSDAY **WORD:** *Nasal*

○ FRIDAY **WORD:** *Numerical*

○ SATURDAY / SUNDAY **WORD:** *BIOLOGY*

5th Grade Word of The Day

Use the dictionary to write the definition
and divide the words for each day
below into syllables.

○ MONDAY   WORD: *Moraine*

Write Words In ABC Order

○ TUESDAY   WORD: *Moisture*

○ WEDNESDAY   WORD: *Millimeter*

For each word, find one synonym
& one antonym.

○ THURSDAY   WORD: *Metaphor*

○ FRIDAY   WORD: *Mercy*

○ SATURDAY / SUNDAY   WORD: *OXYGEN*

5th Grade Word of The Day

Week 11

Use the dictionary to write the definition and divide the words for each day below into syllables.

○ MONDAY **WORD:** *Longitude*

Write Words In ABC Order

_____
_____
_____
_____
_____

○ TUESDAY **WORD:** *Legislative*

_____
_____
_____

○ WEDNESDAY **WORD:** *Latitude*

For each word, find one synonym & one antonym.

_____
_____

○ THURSDAY **WORD:** *Kilometer*

_____
_____
_____
_____

○ FRIDAY **WORD:** *Judicial*

_____
_____
_____

○ SATURDAY / SUNDAY **WORD:** *FREQUENT*

_____
_____
_____

5th Grade Word of The Day

Use the dictionary to write the definition and divide the words for each day below into syllables.

○ MONDAY **WORD:** *Invasion*

Write Words In ABC Order

_____

_____

_____

○ TUESDAY **WORD:** *Inflation*

_____

_____

_____

○ WEDNESDAY **WORD:** *Illusion*

For each word, find one synonym & one antonym.

_____

_____

○ THURSDAY **WORD:** *Iceberg*

_____

_____

_____

_____

○ FRIDAY **WORD:** *Hostile*

_____

_____

_____

○ SATURDAY / SUNDAY **WORD:** *OSTRICH*

_____

_____

_____

5th Grade Word of The Day

Use the dictionary to write the definition and divide the words for each day below into syllables.

○ MONDAY **WORD:** *Hermit*

Write Words In ABC Order

○ TUESDAY **WORD:** *Hemisphere*

○ WEDNESDAY **WORD:** *Glacier*

For each word, find one synonym & one antonym.

○ THURSDAY **WORD:** *Freckle*

○ FRIDAY **WORD:** *Generalize*

○ SATURDAY / SUNDAY **WORD:** *PELICAN*

5th Grade Word of The Day

Use the dictionary to write the definition
and divide the words for each day
below into syllables.

○ MONDAY **WORD:** *Gusher*

Write Words In ABC Order

○ TUESDAY **WORD:** *Habitat*

○ WEDNESDAY **WORD:** *Fragile*

For each word, find one synonym
& one antonym.

○ THURSDAY **WORD:** *Flamingo*

○ FRIDAY **WORD:** *Executive*

○ SATURDAY / SUNDAY **WORD:** *INVISIBLE*

5th Grade Word of The Day

Use the dictionary to write the definition and divide the words for each day below into syllables.

○ MONDAY **WORD:** *Engineer*

Write Words In ABC Order

○ TUESDAY **WORD:** *Emerald*

○ WEDNESDAY **WORD:** *Ecosystem*

For each word, find one synonym & one antonym.

○ THURSDAY **WORD:** *Ecology*

○ FRIDAY **WORD:** *Eclipse*

○ SATURDAY / SUNDAY **WORD:** *WIGWAM*

5th Grade Word of The Day

Use the dictionary to write the definition
and divide the words for each day
below into syllables.

○ MONDAY   **WORD:** *Dimension*

Write Words In ABC Order

○ TUESDAY **WORD:** *Devotion*

○ WEDNESDAY **WORD:** *Decode*

For each word, find one synonym
& one antonym.

○ THURSDAY **WORD:** *Debris*

○ FRIDAY **WORD:** *Customary*

○ SATURDAY / SUNDAY **WORD:** *AUTHENTICITY*

5th Grade Word of The Day

Week 17 — Use the dictionary to write the definition and divide the words for each day below into syllables.

○ MONDAY **WORD:** *Crumble*

Write Words In ABC Order

_____

_____

_____

○ TUESDAY **WORD:** *Council*

_____

_____

_____

_____

○ WEDNESDAY **WORD:** *Continent*

For each word, find one synonym & one antonym.

_____

_____

○ THURSDAY **WORD:** *Conductor*

_____

_____

_____

_____

○ FRIDAY **WORD:** *Comedy*

_____

_____

_____

○ SATURDAY / SUNDAY **WORD:** *GENE*

_____

_____

_____

5th Grade Word of The Day

Week 18

Use the dictionary to write the definition and divide the words for each day below into syllables.

○ MONDAY **WORD:** *Coastal*

Write Words In ABC Order

○ TUESDAY **WORD:** *Citizenship*

○ WEDNESDAY **WORD:** *Cherub*

For each word, find one synonym & one antonym.

○ THURSDAY **WORD:** *Charcoal*

○ FRIDAY **WORD:** *Century*

○ SATURDAY / SUNDAY **WORD:** *ANTIBODY*

5th Grade Word of The Day

Week 19

Use the dictionary to write the definition and divide the words for each day below into syllables.

○ MONDAY   **WORD:** *Centimeter*

Write Words In ABC Order

_____

_____

_____

_____

○ TUESDAY   **WORD:** *Cello*

_____

_____

_____

_____

○ WEDNESDAY **WORD:** *Cartridge*

For each word, find one synonym & one antonym.

_____

○ THURSDAY   **WORD:** *Bureau*

_____

_____

_____

_____

_____

_____

○ FRIDAY   **WORD:** *Bleacher*

_____

_____

_____

_____

○ SATURDAY / SUNDAY   **WORD:** *COMMISSION*

_____

_____

_____

_____

5th Grade Word of The Day

Use the dictionary to write the definition and divide the words for each day below into syllables.

○ MONDAY **WORD:** *Banquet*

Write Words In ABC Order

_____

_____

_____

○ TUESDAY **WORD:** *Ballot*

_____

_____

_____

○ WEDNESDAY **WORD:** *Array*

For each word, find one synonym & one antonym.

_____

○ THURSDAY **WORD:** *Artistic*

_____

_____

_____

_____

○ FRIDAY **WORD:** *Askew*

_____

_____

_____

_____

○ SATURDAY / SUNDAY **WORD:** *BLIZZARD*

_____

_____

_____

5th Grade Word of The Day

Use the dictionary to write the definition and divide the words for each day below into syllables.

○ MONDAY WORDS: *Astronomy*

Write Words In ABC Order

○ TUESDAY WORDS: *Arithmetic*

○ WEDNESDAY WORDS: *Architecture*

For each word, find one synonym & one antonym.

○ THURSDAY WORDS: *Apricot*

○ FRIDAY WORDS: *Antonym*

○ SATURDAY / SUNDAY WORDS: *CALICO*

5th Grade Word of The Day

Use the dictionary to write the definition
and divide the words for each day
below into syllables.

○ MONDAY WORDS: *Aloof*

Write Words In ABC Order

○ TUESDAY WORDS: *Affection*

○ WEDNESDAY WORDS: *Academic*

For each word, find one synonym
& one antonym.

○ THURSDAY WORDS: *Absolute*

○ FRIDAY WORDS: *Browser*

○ SATURDAY / SUNDAY WORDS: *DISTINCT*

5th Grade Word of The Day

Week 23

Use the dictionary to write the definition and divide the words for each day below into syllables.

○ MONDAY **WORDS:** *Brotherhood*

Write Words In ABC Order

_____

_____

○ TUESDAY **WORDS:** *Bridal*

_____

_____

_____

_____

○ WEDNESDAY **WORDS:** *Canvas*

For each word, find one synonym & one antonym.

_____

○ THURSDAY **WORDS:** *Camouflage*

_____

_____

_____

_____

○ FRIDAY **WORDS:** *Carbon*

_____

_____

_____

_____

○ SATURDAY / SUNDAY **WORDS:** *IMPLY*

_____

_____

_____

New Words WordSearch Puzzle

C	I	V	N	I	N	F	E	R	R	E	D	K	J	Z	Z
Z	S	O	L	S	T	I	C	E	J	Y	K	L	W	T	B
N	G	K	T	B	S	I	N	G	L	E	A	N	E	G	Z
E	L	F	R	G	D	E	V	E	L	O	P	I	N	G	G
I	D	E	L	A	W	A	R	E	M	W	V	C	F	S
M	I	S	C	O	N	C	E	P	T	I	O	N	K	S	U
Q	H	H	F	X	E	O	B	S	T	R	U	C	T	R	B
V	U	C	P	R	O	J	E	C	T	I	O	N	T	T	S
R	I	A	G	G	H	P	P	T	M	T	M	V	N	E	C
E	B	G	R	B	H	P	R	I	D	T	F	A	G	N	R
A	G	H	W	T	K	R	O	N	U	R	T	R	G	O	I
L	E	C	O	I	E	N	V	Y	I	S	E	Z	R	I	B
I	B	R	L	M	T	T	I	W	N	M	Y	Z	P	S	E
Z	M	P	V	Q	L	O	D	I	B	J	E	O	M	I	N
E	G	A	E	Q	M	Y	E	U	D	W	P	U	N	L	F
W	B	R	S	A	U	P	S	W	L	L	K	M	T	Y	P

MISCONCEPTION	PROJECTION	PROVIDE	QUARTET	REALIZE
INFERRED	DELAWARE	OBSTRUCT	DEVELOPING	INSTANT
WOLVES	SOLSTICE	SUBMERGE	SUBSCRIBE	SINGLE
NOISILY				

Write sentences using words from above. Look up words when you are uncertain of their meanings.

Learn 1-3 New Words A Day

Please *unscramble* the compound words below.

Rattlesnake	Watchword	Newscaster	Fishhook	Forbid	Nursemaid
Waterfront	Tenderfoot	Fishmonger	Lifeblood	Granddaughter	Blowgun
Forgive	Newsroom	Wheelchair	Forehead		

1. EOIL FDLOB   L _ _ e _ _ _ o _ _

2. IEACRWHELH   W h _ _ l _ _ _ _ _

3. EARKTTLSENA   R _ _ _ _ _ s _ a _ _

4. ERWRFTOATN   _ _ _ e _ _ _ o _ t

5. WNLOGBU   B _ o _ _ _ _

6. OHHKISOF   _ _ _ _ _ _ o k

7. GURAHDGARDNTE   _ _ _ n _ _ _ u _ h _ _ _

8. ONRWMSE O   _ _ _ _ _ _ _ m

9. NOIGHRMSEF   _ i s _ _ _ _ g _ _

10. EVGRIFO   _ o _ g _ _ _

11. IRDOFB   _ o _ _ i _

12. WORHTDWCA   _ a _ _ _ _ o _ _

13. ROFDAEEH   _ _ _ e h _ _ _

14. SESTNRAWCE   N _ w s _ _ _ _ _ _

15. RNAMSUEDI   N _ _ _ _ _ a _ _

16. RONOFETTED   _ _ _ d _ _ _ _ o t

Write sentences using words from above. Look up words when you are uncertain of their meanings.

_____

New Words WordSearch Puzzle

```
H  N  O  R  T  H  E  R  N  F  I  N  A  N  C  E
S  I  N  V  J  X  G  R  E  A  T  E  S  T  T  F
U  N  P  Q  G  J  G  U  L  L  I  B  L  E  O  M
T  H  K  P  K  Y  Z  E  M  I  N  P  N  N  L  T
R  E  C  H  O  F  J  F  N  O  K  E  E  D  E  F
T  E  N  T  H  P  P  A  I  L  L  J  C  W  R  C
F  F  V  Y  P  J  O  T  O  B  H  N  E  R  A  O
I  D  M  Y  Z  R  A  T  A  T  O  E  S  I  T  M
N  U  F  C  W  G  D  T  A  I  T  U  S  D  I  M
A  W  I  F  I  E  A  G  T  M  M  U  A  I  N  I
N  R  X  L  A  B  B  C  H  Z  U  N  R  C  G  T
C  Y  B  M  E  U  U  B  R  V  Y  S  Y  U  A  T
I  O  M  D  H  D  T  T  E  Y  W  D  D  L  W  I
A  J  W  X  O  F  T  U  B  D  E  F  T  O  Y  N
L  K  T  R  R  I  E  I  M  C  O  S  Y  U  B  G
C  P  P  V  D  D  J  Z  V  N  S  I  Y  S  P  G
```

HIPPOPOTAMUS	FINANCE	RIDICULOUS	NECESSARY	NORTHERN
GULLIBLE	DEBATABLE	TENTH	WEBBED	FINANCIAL
GREATEST	AUTUMN	COMMITTING	TOLERATING	PRODUCTION
OBLIGATION				

Write sentences using words from above. Look up words when you are uncertain of their meanings.

....

_____

New Words WordSearch Puzzle

```
X  I  S  U  B  D  I  V  I  S  I  O  N  S  I  H
B  Y  S  M  P  V  O  K  P  V  P  V  U  P  N  E
S  P  Y  H  T  R  A  C  E  M  P  W  C  E  D  R
X  B  B  W  R  G  N  I  T  A  L  Y  O  C  E  I
S  T  R  A  T  O  S  P  H  E  R  E  N  U  F  T
C  D  E  C  L  A  R  A  T  I  O  N  S  L  I  A
G  P  X  D  H  I  B  E  D  K  X  N  C  A  N  G
P  R  L  C  I  C  A  U  G  H  T  D  I  T  I  E
N  I  U  E  O  I  D  C  Z  D  E  P  E  I  T  K
O  K  Z  M  T  K  N  Y  X  K  Y  X  N  N  E  N
O  R  E  C  B  L  N  S  I  Z  H  L  C  G  O  E
D  P  A  H  U  L  F  J  L  I  A  D  E  Z  X  P
L  C  B  N  I  N  E  H  E  F  Y  M  I  K  F  S
E  A  D  J  A  C  E  N  T  L  R  R  X  P  M  B
A  Q  C  H  R  G  T  A  Z  G  O  G  D  Y  G  I
V  I  R  G  I  N  I  A  V  H  F  B  P  S  A  G
```

SPECULATING	CONSCIENCE	SUBDIVISION	ADJACENT	HERITAGE
INDEFINITE	HORIZON	TRACE	NOODLE	ITALY
GRUMBLE	STRATOSPHERE	VIRGINIA	CAUGHT	CACTI
DECLARATION				

Write sentences using words from above. Look up words when you are uncertain of their meanings.

Learn 1-3 New Words A Day

Please *unscramble* the words below.

CONVICT	COMPETITION	ANTISOCIAL	ADHERE	BREAKFAST	COLLIDE
DISLIKE	CALIFORNIA	CONCENTRATION	SIMILAR	ESOPHAGUS	DESCRIPTION
LEOPARD	ENTERED				

1. DAEHRE   _ _ H E _ _

2. AOSUEGHPS   E _ _ P _ _ _ _ _

3. ELDRPOA   _ _ O P _ _ _

4. CTINPOEMTOI   _ O _ _ E _ _ T _ _ _

5. ILOCANRIFA   _ _ _ _ _ _ _ N I A

6. NREEEDT   _ _ _ E _ _ D

7. LLOEDIC   _ O _ _ I _ _

8. ITLCSAOIAN   A _ _ _ _ _ C I _ _

9. VOCCITN   _ O N _ _ _ _

10. RINNCTECOATNO   _ _ N _ _ _ _ _ _ _ I O _

11. IARSILM   _ _ _ I L _ _

12. OCIPRNDIEST   _ E _ _ _ _ _ _ O N

13. KILDSIE   D _ _ _ _ _ E

14. FBKAARSTE   _ _ _ _ K F _ _ _

Write sentences using words from above. Look up words when you are uncertain of their meanings.

Learn 1-3 New Words A Day

Name: _____

Date: _____

Please *unscramble* the words below.

INFRACTION	INTERESTING	IMPROVEMENT	COMMUNICATION	LEVEL	ENJOY
CONSEQUENTLY	ASTRONOMICAL	ALTERNATE	AFRICA	LIBRARY	EXPELLING
ASTRONAUT	SILENT				

1. YABILRR   _ I _ _ A _ _

2. EXNPELLIG   _ X _ E _ _ _ _ _

3. VNMIOEPMERT   I M _ _ _ _ _ _ N _

4. RELNEATAT   A _ T _ _ _ _ _

5. LELVE   L _ _ _ _

6. TIENIGSNETR   _ N _ _ _ _ T I _ _

7. AOTUTRNSA   _ _ T R _ _ _ _ _

8. OUTECEYLNNQS   _ _ _ _ E _ _ _ N _ L _

9. EYOJN   _ N _ _ _

10. FAIRAC   _ _ _ I C _

11. SIELNT   _ _ L E _ _

12. CICTNOOMUAMIN   _ _ M _ _ _ _ _ A _ _ _ N

13. ATLIMSARNOCO   _ _ _ R O _ _ M _ _ _ _

14. AOIFRCNTIN   _ _ _ R _ C _ I _ _

Write sentences using words from above. Look up words when you are uncertain of their meanings.

_____

_____

Learn 1-3 New Words A Day

Name: _____

Date: _____

Please *unscramble* the words below.

TRIPLE	REHEARSE	DISADVANTAGE	REGRETTING	FORTRESS	VICTORY
CRIMINOLOGY	OPPOSITE	RELY	AGREEMENT	GAUGE	CONCEIVE
MYTHOLOGY	COMPLETELY	FURTHERMORE	OCTAVE		

1. EOCENIVC   _ _ _ _ E _ _ E

2. MOTOYLYHG   _ _ T _ _ _ _ G _

3. ERYL   _ _ L _

4. HEFRERTMRUO   _ _ _ _ _ _ _ M O R _

5. ANVEDAGSDITA   _ _ _ _ D _ _ _ T A _ _

6. VCOTEA   _ _ T A _ _

7. EHAERRES   R E _ _ _ _ _ _

8. IOVRTYC   _ I _ T _ _ _

9. PITRLE   _ R _ _ L _

10. GAEUG   _ _ _ G _

11. PSTOPEIO   _ _ P _ S _ _ _

12. GERITTGREN   _ _ _ _ _ T _ _ N G

13. CLPTLYEEOM   _ _ M _ _ E _ _ _ Y

14. MTEERNEAG   _ _ _ _ _ M E _ _

15. SFRSTEOR   _ O _ _ R _ _ _

16. NLIMGIOYORC   _ _ _ M _ _ O _ _ _ Y

Write sentences using words from above. Look up words when you are uncertain of their meanings.

_____

Learn 1-3 New Words A Day

Name: _____

Date: _____

Please *unscramble* the words below.

INTERSTATE	GEOMETRY	MIGRATION	TANGIBLE	SPRINT	ASHAMED
COMPLIANT	IMPROVING	BRANCHES	AUDITORY	COMPANION	TOLERABLE
ANTIBIOTIC	CONDITIONS	SATURN	COMPOSITE		

1. LRLABTEOE   _ _ _ _ _ A B _ _

2. SRNTPI   S _ R _ _ _

3. AOCNMNPOI   _ _ _ _ A _ I _ _

4. ORVIIMPGN   _ _ P _ O _ _ _ _

5. STRUNA   _ _ _ _ R N

6. ARBSNHEC   _ _ _ _ _ H _ S

7. TOESCOPIM   _ O M _ _ _ _ _ _

8. GAETNIBL   T _ N _ _ _ _ _

9. OIAMGNTIR   _ I _ _ _ _ _ O _

10. CTSDIONNOI   _ O _ _ _ T I _ _ _

11. OURATYID   _ U _ _ _ O _ _

12. EDAMASH   _ _ H A _ _ _

13. PNCOTLIAM   _ _ _ _ _ _ _ A _ T

14. NTIOITACIB   _ _ _ _ _ _ I _ T I _

15. TISETNARET   _ _ T _ R _ _ A _ _

16. EGROEMTY   _ E _ _ E _ _ _ _

Write sentences using words from above. Look up words when you are uncertain of their meanings.

_____

_____

_____

_____

_____

Learn 1-3 New Words A Day

Name: _____

Date: _____

Please *unscramble* the words below.

CHOREOGRAPHY	CACTUS	MANDATORY	BRILLIANT	PSYCHOLOGY	FEBRUARY
FRENCH	CONFLICT	WHISPER	DIVISIBLE	TURTLE	CENTENNIAL
COMPOUND	REFERRED	UNUSUAL	BRAZIL		

1. UNUAUSL   _ _ _ S _ A _

2. GEOOHARCHRPY   _ _ O _ _ _ _ R _ _ H _

3. CASCUT   _ _ C T _ _

4. EEFERDRR   _ E _ _ _ _ E _

5. POOGLCYSYH   _ S _ _ H _ _ _ _ Y

6. CCLIOFNT   _ _ _ _ _ _ C T

7. ELURTT   T _ _ _ L _

8. FRBRYUAE   F _ _ _ U _ _ _

9. ANBLLIITR   _ _ _ _ L _ _ N _

10. MODOUNPC   C O _ _ _ _ _ _

11. ABLIRZ   _ R _ _ _ L

12. HFCREN   _ R _ _ _ H

13. IIEBVLSID   _ _ _ I _ I _ _ _

14. INTNALECNE   C E _ _ _ N _ _ _ _

15. RHSIEPW   _ _ _ _ P E _

16. ARADTNMYO   M _ _ _ _ T _ _ _

Write sentences using words from above. Look up words when you are uncertain of their meanings.

_____

Learn 1-3 New Words A Day

Name: _____

Date: _____

Please *unscramble* the words below.

SPAGHETTI	INCREASE	PREFERABLE	POLITICIAN	PICNIC	HORRIBLE
PRACTICE	AMBIENT	NOTABLE	FUNGI	INTERNET	HEADACHE
PERSECUTION	PROTEIN	PUBLICITY	GREEK		

1. OLPIITCNAI   _ _ L _ T _ _ _ _ N

2. HBIORLRE   H _ _ _ _ _ _ E

3. HEACHAED   _ E A _ _ _ _ _

4. BINMAET   A M _ _ _ _ _

5. IBILPUTCY   _ _ B _ I _ _ _ _

6. CPINCI   _ _ _ N I _

7. ANLTOBE   _ _ T _ B _ _

8. UINFG   _ _ N _ _

9. EGREK   _ R _ _ _

10. OESRUPCNITE   _ _ _ _ _ C U _ _ O _

11. NOIREPT   _ _ _ _ E _ N

12. IAEPTSTHG   _ P _ _ H _ _ _

13. ENIRNETT   _ _ T _ _ _ E _

14. ERFLEBEAPR   P _ E _ _ _ A _ _ _

15. CATEPCRI   _ _ _ _ _ I _ E

16. EEINARSC   _ N C _ _ _ _ _

Write sentences using words from above. Look up words when you are uncertain of their meanings.

_____

_____

_____

_____

Learn 1-3 New Words A Day

Please *unscramble* the words below.

YEAST	VELVET	COMMITTEE	EQUINE	TENNESSEE	AUGUST
PANEL	OCTOBER	SUBSTANTIAL	FREIGHT	SENSE	DIMENSIONAL
DEDICATION	COORDINATE	EDITING			

1. SESENEETN   _ _ _ _ E _ _ E _

2. HGETRFI   _ _ _ _ G H _

3. DGNITIE   _ _ I T _ _ _

4. EIMOTETCM   _ _ _ _ I _ _ E _

5. GTAUSU   _ U _ _ S _

6. SSNEE   _ _ _ _ E

7. ERBOCOT   _ _ _ O _ E _

8. ILMSNIDAONE   _ I _ _ N _ _ _ _ L

9. TEAYS   Y _ _ _ _

10. EVTEVL   _ _ L V _ _

11. DTAIICDNEO   _ _ D I _ _ _ _ _ N

12. RTNEODICAO   _ _ _ R _ _ _ A T _

13. NAPEL   _ _ _ E _

14. UEEIQN   E _ _ _ _ E

15. ALSASUBITNT   S _ B _ _ _ N _ _ _ _

Write sentences using words from above. Look up words when you are uncertain of their meanings.

....

....

....

....

Name: _____

Learn 1-3 New Words A Day

Date: _____

Please *unscramble* the words below.

ENVIRONMENT	BRUISE	INFLUENTIAL	DUPLICATE	HIPPOPOTAMI	MERCURY
SUBHEADING	PERISHABLE	CONSTANT	AMBIGUITY	CERTIFICATE	FORGETTING
INFORMATION	ASTROLOGY	MISSISSIPPI			

1. TNACTOSN _ _ _ _ T A _ _

2. PMOPIOTIPHA _ _ _ _ _ _ O T A _ _

3. TAEFTIIRCEC _ _ _ _ I _ I _ _ _ E

4. AEICTLUDP D _ _ L _ _ _ _ _

5. SIMSSPSIIIP _ _ _ S _ _ _ _ _ P I

6. UISBER _ _ _ _ S E

7. RMRCEUY _ _ R _ U _ _

8. IUIFAETNLLN _ _ _ _ _ _ N _ I A _

9. TGOGENRITF _ _ _ _ E T _ _ N _

10. NORIVNTNEME E _ _ _ _ _ N _ _ N _

11. IFNROINTOAM _ _ F _ _ _ _ T I _ _

12. BASDGEHIUN _ _ _ H E _ _ I _ _

13. OTYRASGOL _ S _ _ O _ _ _ _

14. YIUTAMGBI _ _ _ _ _ U _ T _

15. IEPAEBRHSL _ E _ _ _ _ A _ _ E

Write sentences using words from above. Look up words when you are uncertain of their meanings.

_____

_____

_____

_____

Learn 1-3 New Words A Day

Name: _____

Date: _____

Please *unscramble* the words below.

MELON	MISSOURI	ARRIVE	ZOOLOGY	QUARREL	SUGGESTED
SOLEMN	TRILOGY	UPSETTING	PLUGGED	AUDIT	TERRIER
UNIVERSE	COMPLAINT	TANGERINE	EXCELLENT	NEEDLE	

1. GEUDGLP   _ _ U _ _ _ D

2. GOIYTRL   _ _ I _ _ G _

3. RIAREV   _ _ R _ V _

4. NEANTIEGR   _ _ N _ _ _ I _ _

5. TAOLICPMN   _ _ M _ _ _ _ _ T

6. NLDEEE   _ E E _ _ _

7. AUTDI   _ U _ _ _

8. OYOOGLZ   _ O O _ _ _ _

9. TIEERRR   T E _ _ _ _ _

10. SUMOISIR   _ _ _ _ _ U R _

11. UERRQAL   _ U _ R _ _ _

12. TCXEELENL   _ _ _ _ L _ E _ _

13. ETSEUSGDG   _ U _ _ E _ _ _ _

14. LNMEO   M _ _ _ _

15. MSELNO   _ _ _ E _ N

16. INVERESU   _ N _ V _ _ _ _

17. TTUINSEPG   _ _ S _ _ _ I _ _

Write sentences using words from above. Look up words when you are uncertain of their meanings.

....

....

....

....

Name: _____

Date: _____

Learn 1-3 New Words A Day

Please *unscramble* the words below.

TERRIFIED	CONTROLLED	ARCHERY	MASSACHUSETTS	SERVANT	MEDIA
METEOROLOGY	ATTRIBUTE	AERODYNAMIC	SUFFRAGE	GENUINE	APPARENTLY
TROUT	VARIOUS				

1. AMIDE   _ _ D _ _

2. NNEGEIU   _ _ N _ I _ _

3. NRAEPPALYT   A _ _ _ _ E _ _ L _

4. EAUTIBTTR   _ T _ _ _ _ _ T _

5. SAETSSACTSM HU   M _ _ _ A _ _ _ _ _ T _ S

6. HRERYCA   _ _ C _ _ _ Y

7. TRVSNAE   _ _ R _ _ N _

8. RERTDIIEF   T _ _ _ I _ _ _ _

9. VIOUSRA   V _ R _ _ _ _

10. AEIMCRNYODA   A _ _ _ _ Y _ A _ _ _

11. ROTECLOLDN   _ _ _ T _ _ L _ _ D

12. RUTTO   _ _ _ _ T

13. FFESGU AR   _ U _ _ _ G _

14. OGEELRYOM OT   _ _ T _ _ R O _ _ _ _

Write sentences using words from above. Look up words when you are uncertain of their meanings.

Spelling Genius Word Study

Spell each of your words by looking carefully at the spelling, covering the word up (with paper) and then try to write it by yourself two times.

VETERAN	VIDEO	VIEW	VILLAIN	VIOLIN

VOUCHER	VOWEL	VULTURE	WALL	WASHER

WASHES	WEEKLY	WELT	WHALE	WHIP

WHIRL	WHISTLE	WIDE	WILT	WINGS

Spelling Genius Word Study

Spell each of your words by looking carefully at the spelling, covering the word up (with paper) and then try to write it by yourself two times.

WINK	WISHES	WOMAN	WORKERS	WORLD	WAGON

WEDGE	WHINE	WHOM	WIGWAM	WINDOW	WITHIN

WOLVES	WOODLAND	WRENCH	WRITTEN	YEAR	YESTERDAY

YOURSELF	YOUTH	ACCOUNT	ACTION	ACTUALLY	ADAPT

AIRPLANE	AIRY	ALMOST	ALONG	ALOUD	ALWAYS

Spelling Genius Word Study

Spell each of your words by looking carefully at the spelling, covering the word up (with paper) and then try to write it by yourself two times.

AMONG	AMOUNT	ANNOY	ANSWER	APPEARANCE

APRON	ARCTIC	AREA	ARGUMENT	ARMY

AROUND	ATOMIC	AUDIENCE	AUTHOR	AVAILABLE

AXLE	BADGE	BALCONY	BALLOON	BARE

Spelling Genius Word Study

Spell each of your words by looking carefully at the spelling, covering the word up (with paper) and then try to write it by yourself two times.

BARTER	BASEBALL	BASKET	BATCH	BAYOU

BEAR	BEAUTIFUL	BEGAN	BEGIN	BEHAVIOR

BEHIND	BELONG	BETTER	BETWEEN	BIGGER

BIRDS	BLOOD	BOARD	BOOKCASE	BORDER

BORED	BORN	BOTTLES	BOUGHT

Spelling Genius Word Study

Spell each of your words by looking carefully at the spelling, covering the word up (with paper) and then try to write it by yourself two times.

BOUNTIFUL	BROKE	BUFFALO	BURNED	BURST

BUTTERFLY	BUYING	CABIN	CALCULATE	CANDLE

CANNOT	CAPABLE	CAREFULLY	CARPET	CARRIED

CARRY	CELLAR	CENTER	CENTRAL	CHANCE

CHECKED	CHEERFUL	CHOICE	CHOOSE	CHUCKLE

Spelling Genius Word Study

Spell each of your words by looking carefully at the spelling, covering the word up (with paper) and then try to write it by yourself two times.

CHURCH	CITRUS	CIVIL	CLARIFY	CLASSROOM

CLEAR	CLERK	CLIMATE	CLOSE	CLOUD

COLLECT	COLORFUL	COMBINATION	COMMON	COMPARE

COMPLEX	CONDOR	CONDUCT	CONFESSION	CONSTITUTION

CONTINUITY	CONTRAST	COPY	CORRECT	COUNTRY

Name _____

Date _____

Spelling Genius Word Study

Spell each of your words by looking carefully at the spelling, covering the word up (with paper) and then try to write it by yourself two times.

COWBOY	CRASH	CRAWL	CRIED	CROSS

CROWN	CULTURE	CURLED	CURRENT	CURTAIN

CUSTOM	CYCLE	DANCE	DANGEROUSLY	DATA

DAWN	DECIMAL	DELTA	DENOMINATOR	DESERT

Spelling Genius Word Study

Spell each of your words by looking carefully at the spelling, covering the word up (with paper) and then try to write it by yourself two times.

DIFFERENCE	DIFFERENT	DISAPPEAR	DISCOVERY	DISPOSABLE

DISTANCE	DITCH	DIVING	DRIED	DROUGHT

EARTH	EAST	EASY	ELAPSE	ELECTRIC

ELLIPTICAL	ELSE	EMPTIED	EMPTY	ENGINE

Spelling Genius Word Study

Spell each of your words by looking carefully at the spelling, covering the word up (with paper) and then try to write it by yourself two times.

ERASABLE	ESPECIALLY	ESTABLISH	EVERY	EVERYONE

EXACT	EXAMPLE	EXPLORER	EXPRESS	EXTINCT

FAIRY	FAMILIES	FAMILY	FEATURE	FEDERAL

FEELING	FENCE	FEVER	FINAL	FIRM

FLOUR	FLOWER	FOCUS	FOLKLORE	FOLLOW

Name _____

Date _____

Spelling Genius Word Study

Spell each of your words by looking carefully at the spelling, covering the word up (with paper) and then try to write it by yourself two times.

FOOTBALL	FOREST	FORMALLY	FORMULA	FOUNTAIN

FOURTH	FRACTION	FRONT	FUTURE	GARDEN

GENERAL	GENTLE	GEOGRAPHY	GIGGLE	GINGER

GIRAFFE	GLARE	GOVERNMENT	GRAND	GROUND

Spelling Genius Word Study

Spell each of your words by looking carefully at the spelling, covering the word up (with paper) and then try to write it by yourself two times.

GROWL	GUILTY	GUN	HAIR	HALLWAY

HANDLE	HAPPIEST	HARE	HARMFUL	HELD

HELPFULLY	HIGH	HIGHEST	HIGHWAY	HISTORY

HOMETOWN	HONORABLY	HOTTER	HOWEVER	HUGGED

HUNDRED	HUNTING	HURRIED	ICING	IDEA

Spelling Genius Word Study

Spell each of your words by looking carefully at the spelling, covering the word up (with paper) and then try to write it by yourself two times.

IMPORTANT	IMPROPER	INCHES	INDEPENDENCE	INTERACT

INTERACTION	IRON	IRRITABLY	IVORY	JERKED

JOYFULLY	JUMPED	JURY	KNEE	KNIFE

KNOCK	KNOT	KNOWLEDGE	KNOWN	LADY

LASSO	LAUGHABLE	LAUGHED	LAUNDRY	LAWYER

Circle the correct spelling.

	A	B	C	D
1.	Adae	Adage	Adadge	Adea
2.	Axiss	Axisc	Axis	Axas
3.	Course	Courrse	Coorse	Coorrse
4.	Crrocodile	Crocodile	Crucodile	Crrucodile
5.	Fiftean	Fifteen	Fiften	Fiphten
6.	Fourten	Fourteen	Foorten	Fourtean
7.	Habattat	Habitat	Habatat	Habittat
8.	Ilegal	Ilegil	Illegil	Illegal
9.	Damage	Damadge	Damea	Damae
10.	Cusctomary	Customary	Costomary	Cusstomary
11.	Generite	Generrite	Generate	Generrate
12.	Advine	Advence	Advane	Advance
13.	Catle	Citle	Cittle	Cattle
14.	Flamingo	Flamingu	Fllamingu	Fllamingo
15.	Fiqed	Filled	Falled	Faled
16.	Carve	Cirve	Carrve	Cirrve
17.	Eighten	Eaghten	Eighteen	Eightean
18.	Contact	Conttact	Cuntact	Cunttact
19.	Corruption	Coruption	Coruptoin	Corruptoin
20.	Cible	Cablle	Cable	Ciblle
21.	College	Colege	Coleje	Colleje
22.	Bleacher	Blleacher	Blaecher	Bllaecher

23.	Bellieve	Believe	Belleive	Beleive
24.	Emotoin	Emottoin	Emottion	Emotion
25.	Brraket	Brracket	Bracket	Braket
26.	Anttunym	Antonym	Antunym	Anttonym
27.	Commute	Commoye	Comote	Comute
28.	Coasstal	Cuastal	Coasctal	Coastal
29.	Ellevatur	Elevator	Elevatur	Ellevator
30.	Ecousystem	Ecoussystem	Ecosystem	Ecossystem
31.	Errosoin	Erosoin	Errosion	Erosion
32.	Equation	Equattion	Equattoin	Equatoin
33.	Ankle	Anckle	Anklle	Anckle
34.	Although	Althoogh	Allthough	Allthoogh
35.	Dral	Drill	Drall	Dril
36.	Cinyn	Canyun	Canyon	Canyn
37.	Complete	Cumpllete	Compllete	Cumplete
38.	Envelope	Envellupe	Envelupe	Envellope
39.	Against	Againsst	Agiansst	Agianst
40.	Depossit	Deposit	Depousit	Depoussit
41.	Early	Eirrly	Eirly	Earrly
42.	Fittal	Fatal	Fattal	Fital
43.	Earrthqauke	Earthquake	Earrthquake	Earthqauke
44.	Deparrtore	Departure	Deparrture	Departore
45.	Fixture	Fixtture	Fixttore	Fixtore
46.	Crreature	Creature	Craeture	Crraeture
47.	Guest	Guesst	Guesct	Goest
48.	Buglle	Boglle	Bomle	Bugle
49.	Bandae	Bandadge	Bandea	Bandage
50.	Dolfin	Dolphin	Dollfin	Dollphin
51.	Corrner	Corner	Currner	Curner

52.	Dissruption	Dissruptoin	Disruptoin	Disruption
53.	Abuce	Abuse	Abusse	Abusce
54.	Guldei	Gollden	Golden	Gullden
55.	Depresion	Depresoin	Depressoin	Depression
56.	Cherrob	Cherub	Cherob	Cherrub
57.	Continent	Conttinent	Cuntinent	Cunttinent
58.	Himmer	Hamer	Hammer	Himer
59.	Contain	Contian	Conttian	Conttain
60.	Dictoinary	Dicttionary	Dictionary	Dicttoinary
61.	Dimension	Dimensoin	Dimenssion	Dimenssoin
62.	Image	Imea	Imae	Imadge
63.	Frame	Frrame	Frrime	Frime
64.	Aloph	Alof	Aloof	Alouf
65.	Diamond	Daimond	Daimund	Diamund
66.	Becime	Became	Becea	Becae
67.	Congresc	Congres	Cungres	Congress
68.	Canun	Cajon	Cannun	Cannon
69.	Energy	Enarrgy	Enerrgy	Enargy
70.	Gllobe	Glube	Globe	Gllube
71.	Chipell	Chipel	Chapell	Chapel
72.	Carrot	Carrut	Carut	Carot
73.	Forward	Forrward	Furward	Furrward
74.	Anyue	Anyone	Anyoe	Anyune
75.	Ecullogy	Ecology	Eculogy	Ecollogy
76.	Compotter	Computer	Computter	Compoter
77.	Demid	Demad	Demand	Demind
78.	Capttore	Captture	Captore	Capture
79.	Bobbre	Bubble	Boble	Buble
80.	Deit	Diett	Deitt	Diet

81.	Cautoin	Caution	Cauttoin	Cauttion
82.	Clluase	Cllause	Cluase	Clause
83.	Charge	Charrje	Charje	Charrge
84.	Galun	Galon	Gallon	Gallun
85.	Guscher	Gosher	Gussher	Gusher
86.	Aprricot	Aprricut	Apricot	Apricut
87.	Cromble	Crromble	Crumble	Crrumble
88.	Generralize	Generralaze	Generalaze	Generalize
89.	Eaghtty	Eightty	Eighty	Eaghty
90.	Devottoin	Devottion	Devotion	Devotoin
91.	Hosband	Husband	Hussband	Huscband
92.	Cabadge	Cabage	Cabbadge	Cabbage
93.	Allone	Allune	Alune	Alone
94.	Eather	Either	Eatther	Eitther
95.	Disstractoin	Distraction	Distractoin	Disstraction
96.	Adventore	Adventtore	Adventture	Adventure
97.	Coulldn'T	Coolldn'T	Cooldn'T	Couldn'T
98.	Browser	Brrowcer	Browcer	Brrowser
99.	Gurilla	Gorilla	Gurila	Gorila
100.	Boasst	Boasct	Boast	Buast
101.	Evill	Evil	Evall	Eval
102.	Apiont	Appoint	Apoint	Appiont
103.	Frekle	Freckle	Frreckle	Frrekle
104.	Academc	Academac	Academic	Acidemc
105.	Glacier	Glaceir	Gllaceir	Gllacier
106.	Ellectracity	Ellectricity	Electracity	Electricity
107.	Cookies	Cokies	Cookeis	Cokeis
108.	Cirqoe	Cirque	Cirrqoe	Cirrque
109.	Havd	Herd	Harrd	Herrd

110.	Allarm	Alirm	Allirm	Alarm
111.	Averadge	Average	Averrage	Averradge
112.	Calendar	Callendar	Cilendar	Cillendar
113.	Decei	Decie	Debade	Decide
114.	Across	Acrous	Acrouss	Acros
115.	Bllanket	Blancket	Bllancket	Blanket
116.	Heivy	Heavy	Haevy	Hievy
117.	Cruwd	Crruwd	Crowd	Crrowd
118.	Duett	Duet	Doet	Doett
119.	Australai	Australia	Ausstralai	Ausstralia
120.	Eclipce	Eclipse	Ecllipce	Ecllipse
121.	Bitter	Bater	Bieer	Battee
122.	Credat	Crredat	Crredit	Credit
123.	Assia	Asai	Asia	Asoai
124.	Anything	Anythang	Anytthang	Anytthing
125.	Cartun	Carrton	Carrtun	Carton
126.	Exercise	Exerrcise	Exercice	Exerrcice
127.	Executive	Execotive	Executtive	Execottive
128.	Furrty	Furty	Forty	Forrty
129.	Character	Chirracter	Chiracter	Charracter
130.	Becoe	Become	Becue	Becume
131.	Brooght	Brought	Brrooght	Brrought
132.	Chain	Chaan	Chag	Chian
133.	Compasoin	Compassoin	Compasion	Compassion
134.	Friend	Frriend	Frreind	Freind
135.	Factury	Facttory	Facttury	Factory
136.	Elacted	Elected	Ellacted	Ellected
137.	Councill	Cooncil	Council	Cooncill
138.	Carrtridge	Carrtridje	Cartridje	Cartridge

139.	English	Engllish	Englash	Engllash
140.	Breeze	Beaze	Breze	Breaze
141.	Banquett	Banqoett	Banqoet	Banquet
142.	Camoufflage	Camoofflage	Camooflage	Camouflage
143.	Colon	Collon	Cullon	Culon
144.	Architecture	Arrchitectore	Architectore	Arrchitecture
145.	Grapefruit	Grrapephruit	Grrapefruit	Grapephruit
146.	Compas	Compass	Cumpas	Compasc
147.	Hippened	Happened	Hipened	Hapened
148.	Chikn	Chickn	Chicken	Chiken
149.	Garbadge	Garrbage	Garbage	Garrbadge
150.	Dorring	During	Durring	Doring
151.	Fotprint	Foutprint	Footprint	Futprint
152.	Garlac	Garlic	Garrlic	Garrlac
153.	Barel	Birrel	Birel	Barrel
154.	Caraige	Cariage	Carraige	Carriage
155.	Discuk	Discuss	Dissuss	Dissus
156.	Feild	Feilld	Field	Fielld
157.	Deped	Daped	Depend	Dapend
158.	Cqaw	Crew	Crrew	Crraw
159.	Deseive	Deceive	Desieve	Decieve
160.	Consstructoin	Consstruction	Construction	Constructoin
161.	Binaa	Banana	Binana	Banaa
162.	Fuallt	Fault	Fualt	Faullt
163.	Cuper	Cuoper	Copper	Coqer
164.	Absolote	Abscolute	Absolute	Abssolute
165.	Boilding	Boillding	Building	Buillding
166.	Crusher	Crrosher	Crrusher	Crosher
167.	Comay	Comedy	Comey	Cumedy

168.	Boton	Button	Botton	Buton
169.	Brass	Brasc	Bfas	Bris
170.	Fllisher	Flisher	Fllasher	Flasher
171.	Everythang	Everrything	Everrythang	Everything
172.	Asskew	Askew	Asckew	Aske
173.	Crrust	Crrost	Crost	Crust
174.	Cittcher	Catcher	Citcher	Cattcher
175.	Celebrite	Cellebrate	Cellebrite	Celebrate
176.	Debrris	Debrras	Debris	Debras
177.	Balut	Ballut	Ballot	Balot
178.	Cuach	Coah	Cuah	Coach
179.	Hallph	Hallf	Half	Halph
180.	Brroken	Broken	Brocken	Brrocken
181.	Heard	Hearrd	Haerd	Haerrd
182.	Bandit	Banditt	Bandat	Bandatt
183.	Complletion	Completion	Completoin	Complletoin
184.	Bradal	Brradal	Bridal	Brridal
185.	Citizenship	Catizenship	Cattizenship	Cittizenship
186.	Forse	Forrse	Force	Forrce
187.	Chinnel	Chinel	Chanel	Channel
188.	Conservatoin	Consservation	Consservatoin	Conservation
189.	Dagital	Digital	Digittal	Dagittal
190.	Eorope	Eorrope	Eurrope	Europe
191.	Camerra	Cimerra	Camera	Cimera
192.	Composse	Compouse	Compousse	Compose
193.	Actur	Acttur	Acttor	Actor
194.	Engineer	Enginear	Enginer	Enganer
195.	Iceberrg	Iseberg	Iseberrg	Iceberg
196.	Digesstion	Digesstoin	Digestion	Digestoin

Name: _____

Date: _____

Circle the correct spelling.

	A	B	C	D
1.	Magenta	Magentta	Madgentta	Madgenta
2.	Ambivallent	Ambavallent	Ambavalent	Ambivalent
3.	Clif	Cliphf	Cliph	Cliff
4.	Inephective	Ineffective	Inefective	Inephfective
5.	Milionth	Millionth	Millointh	Milointh
6.	Plaster	Pllister	Pllaster	Plister
7.	Permissible	Permissable	Permisable	Permisible
8.	Fasshoin	Fasshion	Fashion	Fashoin
9.	Efect	Effect	Ephfect	Ephect
10.	Wissonsin	Wisssonsin	Wissconsin	Wisconsin
11.	Huricane	Horricane	Horicane	Hurricane
12.	Aodittorium	Aoditorium	Auditorium	Audittorium
13.	Generation	Generration	Generratoin	Generatoin
14.	Awkward	Awkwarrd	Awckwarrd	Awckward
15.	Strinjent	Sttringent	Stringent	Sttrinjent
16.	Sttandard	Standard	Sttindard	Stindard
17.	Insect	Inscect	Inssect	Incect
18.	Hydrojen	Hydrogen	Hydrrojen	Hydrrogen
19.	Cunsonant	Consonant	Conssonant	Consconant
20.	Bacycle	Bicycle	Bicyclle	Bacyclle
21.	Dissatisfeid	Disatisfied	Dissatisfied	Disatisfeid
22.	Eadglle	Eagle	Eaglle	Eadgle

23.	Lavenderr	Lavender	Livenderr	Livender
24.	Plleasant	Plaesant	Pleasant	Pllaesant
25.	Chronology	Chrrunology	Chrronology	Chrunology
26.	Aprentise	Apprentice	Apprentise	Aprentice
27.	Cumparison	Comparrison	Cumparrison	Comparison
28.	Conventoin	Conventtoin	Conventtion	Convention
29.	Performance	Perrformence	Performence	Perrformance
30.	Adjourrn	Adjoorn	Adjoorrn	Adjourn
31.	Decepttoin	Decepttion	Deception	Deceptoin
32.	Speciphic	Speciphfic	Specific	Speciffic
33.	Calloreis	Callories	Calories	Caloreis
34.	Saucer	Saucerr	Suacerr	Suacer
35.	Technaqe	Technique	Techniqe	Techniqoe
36.	Graduate	Grradaute	Gradaute	Grraduate
37.	Connectoin	Conection	Conectoin	Connection
38.	Expllaining	Expllianing	Explianing	Explaining
39.	Catthedral	Cithedral	Citthedral	Cathedral
40.	Theology	Theullogy	Theollogy	Theulogy
41.	Functtoin	Function	Functoin	Functtion
42.	Raciall	Racaill	Racail	Racial
43.	Mexio	Mexicu	Mexico	Mexoi
44.	Bactteria	Bacteria	Bacterai	Bactterai
45.	Someone	Sumeoe	Sumeone	Someoe
46.	Affriad	Afraid	Affraid	Afriad
47.	Disscard	Discard	Disssard	Dissard
48.	Forrecast	Furecast	Furrecast	Forecast
49.	Cullate	Culate	Colate	Collate
50.	Aerrousol	Aerrosol	Aerousol	Aerosol
51.	Adapttation	Adaptatoin	Adaptation	Adapttatoin

52.	Awirre	Awire	Aware	Awarre
53.	Repllacang	Repllacing	Replacang	Replacing
54.	Mercilesc	Merciless	Merciles	Mercales
55.	Forrmation	Formatoin	Forrmatoin	Formation
56.	Busines	Bosines	Business	Businesc
57.	Dominatoin	Dominattion	Dominattoin	Domination
58.	Dellivery	Dellavery	Delivery	Delavery
59.	Reverrent	Reverent	Raverrent	Raverent
60.	Audittion	Audittoin	Auditoin	Audition
61.	Aplacant	Aplicant	Applicant	Applacant
62.	Octtupi	Octopi	Octupi	Octtopi
63.	Luaghter	Luaghtter	Laughtter	Laughter
64.	Cycllone	Cyclone	Cyclune	Cycllune
65.	Qaudrant	Qaudrrant	Quadrrant	Quadrant
66.	Sociollogy	Socoillogy	Socoilogy	Sociology
67.	Apral	Aprril	April	Aprral
68.	Anaul	Annual	Annaul	Anual
69.	Gallop	Galup	Galoz	Gallup
70.	Hyea	Hyae	Hyeni	Hyena
71.	Inelligable	Ineligable	Ineligible	Inelligible
72.	Elves	Ellves	Ellvas	Elvas
73.	Sufering	Suphfering	Suphering	Suffering
74.	Canaa	Cinaa	Cinada	Canada
75.	Aprecaite	Appreciate	Apprecaite	Aprecaite
76.	Aucttion	Auction	Auctoin	Aucttoin
77.	Descign	Design	Dessign	Desagn
78.	Plunje	Pllunje	Plunge	Pllunge
79.	Inscult	Inssult	Insult	Insolt
80.	Gaseoos	Gasseous	Gaseous	Gasseoos

81.	Surprise	Surprice	Surrprise	Surrprice
82.	Tortiose	Tortoise	Torrtoise	Torrtiose
83.	Concessoin	Concesion	Concession	Concesoin
84.	Conttianer	Conttainer	Container	Contianer
85.	Tumble	Tomblle	Tomble	Tumblle
86.	Application	Applicatoin	Aplicatoin	Aplication
87.	Transfer	Transpher	Trranspher	Trransfer
88.	Anceint	Anceintt	Ancientt	Ancient
89.	Cullonel	Collonel	Culonel	Colonel
90.	Torrential	Torrentail	Torentail	Torential
91.	Cartoon	Cartoun	Carson	Cartun
92.	Voyadge	Voyage	Voyea	Voyae
93.	Audable	Audiblle	Aodiblle	Audible
94.	Estimate	Esctimate	Estamate	Esstimate
95.	Methodology	Methudology	Metthudology	Metthodology
96.	Duplex	Dopllex	Doplex	Dupllex
97.	Ethnacity	Etthnicity	Etthnacity	Ethnicity
98.	Ronning	Roning	Runing	Running
99.	Thermousphere	Therrmousphere	Therrmosphere	Thermosphere
100.	Aheid	Ahead	Ahied	Ahaed
101.	Suply	Supply	Sopply	Soply
102.	Carbuhydrates	Carrbohydrates	Carbohydrates	Carrbuhydrates
103.	Patthulogy	Pathulogy	Pathology	Patthology
104.	Abacuss	Abacus	Abacusc	Abacos
105.	Luyall	Loyal	Loyall	Luyal
106.	Ignurrant	Ignorrant	Ignorant	Ignurant
107.	Dephfendant	Deffendant	Dephendant	Defendant
108.	Freeze	Fraze	Freaze	Freze
109.	Sustianed	Sustained	Susstianed	Susstained

110.	Submarrine	Submarine	Sobmarrine	Sobmarine
111.	Invesctigating	Investagating	Investigating	Invesstigating
112.	Experience	Experreince	Experrience	Expereince
113.	Jewellry	Jawelry	Jewelry	Jawellry
114.	Explanatoin	Explanation	Expllanatoin	Expllanation
115.	Capacatty	Capacitty	Capacaty	Capacity
116.	Create	Craete	Crreate	Crraete
117.	Laonch	Launc	Luanch	Launch
118.	Beije	Bieje	Beige	Biege
119.	Typhoon	Typhoun	Tyfon	Typhon
120.	Exchange	Exchine	Exchane	Exchanje
121.	Insurance	Insurence	Inssurance	Inssurence
122.	Arrtacle	Artacle	Article	Arrticle
123.	Cheiff	Chieff	Cheif	Chief
124.	Auttoboigraphy	Auttobiography	Autobiography	Autoboigraphy
125.	Prreposition	Prepositoin	Prrepositoin	Preposition
126.	Ambidexttroos	Ambidexttrous	Ambidextroos	Ambidextrous
127.	September	Septtember	Saptember	Sapttember
128.	Grafic	Grrafic	Graphic	Grraphic
129.	Respiratory	Resspiratory	Respiratury	Rescpiratory
130.	Sollution	Sollutoin	Solution	Solutoin
131.	Prrejudice	Prejudice	Prrejudise	Prejudise
132.	Excatting	Exciting	Excating	Excitting
133.	Incredible	Incredable	Incrredable	Incrredible
134.	Anttidote	Antidute	Antidote	Anttidute
135.	Inaccurate	Inaccorate	Inacurate	Inacorate
136.	Ambittoin	Ambittion	Ambition	Ambitoin
137.	Pallatial	Pallatail	Palatial	Palatail
138.	Nottiphy	Notify	Notiphy	Nottify

139.	Conttest	Contest	Cunttest	Cuntest
140.	Actras	Actres	Actress	Actresc
141.	Collection	Colection	Collectoin	Colectoin
142.	Arrey	Arey	Aray	Array
143.	Heaven	Hieven	Haeven	Heiven
144.	Harbur	Harbor	Harrbor	Harrbur
145.	Courage	Courrage	Coorage	Coorrage
146.	Covered	Cuverred	Coverred	Cuvered
147.	Coment	Comment	Conment	Comnment
148.	Imatate	Imittate	Imitate	Imattate
149.	Hotel	Hottel	Huttel	Hutel
150.	Gerbal	Gerbil	Gerrbal	Gerrbil
151.	Denttil	Denttal	Dental	Dennil
152.	Fosil	Fousil	Foussil	Fossil
153.	Elbow	Ellbuw	Ellbow	Elbuw
154.	Disspersal	Discpersal	Dispersal	Daspersal
155.	Adoptoin	Adopttion	Adopttoin	Adoption
156.	Figore	Figure	Figorre	Figurre
157.	Casstle	Castle	Casctle	Cistle
158.	Frrasher	Frasher	Fresher	Frresher
159.	Decode	Decude	Decue	Decoe
160.	Compatable	Compattable	Compatible	Compattible
161.	Calph	Calf	Callph	Callf
162.	Haerrt	Hearrt	Heart	Haert
163.	Homeworrk	Homeworrck	Homework	Homeworck
164.	Celu	Cellu	Cello	Celo
165.	Bakpack	Backpack	Bakpak	Backpak
166.	Arrathmetic	Arathmetic	Arithmetic	Arrithmetic
167.	Explian	Expllain	Expllian	Explain

168.	Acrrylac	Acrrylic	Acrylac	Acrylic
169.	Hosstile	Housstile	Hostile	Houstile
170.	Clousure	Cllousure	Cllosure	Closure
171.	Brutherhod	Brotherhod	Brotherhoud	Brotherhood
172.	Imatore	Immatore	Imature	Immature
173.	Ellaven	Elaven	Elleven	Eleven
174.	Gadget	Gadgett	Gagett	Gaget
175.	Herrmit	Hermit	Hermat	Herrmat
176.	Barry	Berry	Bery	Bary
177.	Asstronomy	Asctronomy	Astrunomy	Astronomy
178.	Hundredths	Hondrredths	Hundrredths	Hondredths
179.	Bargain	Barrgain	Barrgian	Bargian
180.	Dettermane	Determine	Dettermine	Determane
181.	Charcual	Charrcual	Charrcoal	Charcoal
182.	Bridje	Brridge	Bridge	Brridje
183.	Bosan	Bassin	Bascin	Basin
184.	Devellup	Develop	Develup	Devellop
185.	Artistic	Arrtistic	Artastic	Arrtastic
186.	Balence	Ballence	Balance	Ballance
187.	Cuton	Coton	Cotton	Cutton
188.	Frresh	Fresh	Frrash	Frash
189.	Allraedy	Alraedy	Allready	Already
190.	Disstrict	Disctrict	District	Dastrict
191.	Drima	Drrama	Drama	Drrima
192.	Habatt	Habit	Habitt	Habat
193.	Corona	Curona	Currona	Corrona
194.	Desstroy	Desctroy	Destruy	Destroy
195.	Fluding	Flouding	Flooding	Floding
196.	Callm	Cillm	Cilm	Calm

Name: _____

Date: _____

Learn 1-3 New Words A Day

Please *unscramble* the words below.

PREVENTION	INSPECTION	MAGNETIC	SIXTY	REVISE	PREACHER
SIGNATURE	LANGUAGE	LITERATURE	PUPIL	PIONEER	PROVERB
SCIENTIST	POISON	PERMANENT	PERISH	REACTION	MATHEMATICS
KEPT	MINIATURE				

1. PTKE   _ E _ _

2. PPLIU   P _ _ _ _

3. SXIYT   _ I _ _ _

4. TRPNOVINEE   _ _ _ V E N _ _ _ _

5. RNAPETMNE   _ _ _ _ _ _ E N _

6. SMTEMTCIAAH   M _ T H _ _ _ _ _ _ _

7. SOOPNI   _ _ _ _ O N

8. MINTCEGA   _ _ G N _ _ _ _

9. RVEOPRB   P _ O _ _ _ _

10. INOTAREC   _ E A _ _ _ _ _

11. EROPINE   _ I _ _ E _ _

12. SEIHRP   P E _ _ _ _

13. TETRAILURE   L I _ _ _ A _ _ _ _

14. OETISNCIPN   _ _ S _ E _ T _ _ _

15. ULEAGGNA   L _ _ _ _ _ _ E

16. HECPERRA   P _ _ _ _ _ E _

17. UNRMAIETI   _ _ _ I _ _ _ R _

18. ESSTCNTII   _ _ _ _ N _ _ _ T

19. IEVERS   R _ _ I _ _

20. ATNSGEIRU   _ I _ _ _ _ _ R _

Write sentences using words from above. Look up words when you are uncertain of their meanings.

Learn 1-3 New Words A Day

Please *unscramble* the words below.

RICHER	INFECTION	LEGISLATIVE	PERCENT	PLENTY	PROFESSION
MONITOR	PARSLEY	SHORTEN	REPRESENT	NEUTRAL	REMEMBER
RECYCLE	RESIST	SLIDE	POLLUTION	PASSAGE	RELAX
MITTEN	PERPENDICULAR				

1. EENPRCT   P _ _ _ E _ _

2. EIROONFSSP   _ R _ _ _ _ _ I O _

3. UPINEEADLRRPC   P _ _ _ _ _ _ _ _ _ _ A R

4. NRSPETEER   _ _ _ _ E _ _ N _

5. SEGPAAS   _ _ _ S _ G _

6. CREHIR   _ I _ _ E _

7. REMEBMRE   _ _ M _ M _ _ _

8. RUNELAT   _ E _ _ _ _ L

9. RNSHOET   _ _ O _ T _ _

10. EALXR   R _ _ _ _

11. METTNI   _ I T _ _ _

12. RTSISE   _ _ _ I _ T

13. ALSRYEP   _ _ _ S _ E _

14. EILILEVGATS   _ _ _ _ _ L _ _ I _ E

15. NITPOULLO   _ _ L _ _ _ _ O _

16. NONEICITF   _ _ _ E _ _ _ O _

17. LIDES   _ _ _ _ E

18. ELECCYR   _ E C _ _ _ _

19. ETNLPY   P _ _ N _ _

20. MOINROT   _ _ _ _ T _ R

Write sentences using words from above. Look up words when you are uncertain of their meanings.

_____

_____

_____

_____

_____

_____

_____

_____

_____

_____

_____

_____

_____

_____

Learn 1-3 New Words A Day

Please *unscramble* the words below.

REQUEST	IRRITATION	NEGATIVE	MEMBER	NEITHER	SHOWN
RACCOON	NORMAL	RUPTURE	PLEASURE	MINUS	PARTRIDGE
PARALLEL	SITE	QUANTITY	PROGRAM	NASAL	QUEEN
RABBIT	QUITE				

1. RLNMOA   N _ _ _ A _

2. NERITHE   _ _ _ T H _ _

3. NCORAOC   _ _ _ _ O O _

4. BTIBRA   _ _ _ B I _

5. AIGENVET   _ _ _ _ T I _ _

6. TISE   S _ _ _

7. UQNEE   _ _ _ _ N

8. EBMREM   _ _ _ B _ R

9. UINMS   _ _ N _ _

10. RPESEALU   _ _ _ A _ U _ _

11. DRGARTIEP   _ A _ _ _ _ _ G _

12. ANSAL   _ _ S _ _

13. UPRUETR   _ U _ T _ _ _

14. TNQTAUYI   _ _ _ _ T _ _ Y

15. ESREUQT   _ E _ _ _ S _

16. TQUEI   _ _ _ T _

17. OMPRGRA   _ _ _ _ R _ M

18. OSHNW   _ H _ _ _

19. LPALRALE   _ _ R _ _ _ E _

20. RTOIANRTII   _ R _ _ _ _ T _ _ N

Write sentences using words from above. Look up words when you are uncertain of their meanings.

....

....

Learn 1-3 New Words A Day

Name: _____

Date: _____

Please *unscramble* the words below.

SEVERAL	REPTILE	LEMON	STAMPEDE	REJECT	SENTENCE
REPRODUCE	MILLIMETER	SEQUENCE	SLOWLY	JUVENILE	KNUCKLE
LATITUDE	PRESENTATION	LITER	RELEASE	MONKEY	PUPPET
MOVEMENT	REALLY				

1. ELERSAV   S E _ _ _ _ _

2. ENENSTCE   _ _ _ T E _ _ _

3. ETNPTASIROEN   _ _ _ _ _ _ _ _ _ I O N

4. SLLYWO   _ L _ _ L _

5. MLIELMIETR   _ I _ L _ M _ _ _ _

6. ENMMETVO   _ _ _ E _ _ N _

7. EUSNECQE   _ E _ _ _ _ C _

8. NYKEOM   _ _ N _ E _

9. UJEINVEL   _ U _ _ _ _ E

10. LALRYE   R E _ _ _ _

11. LSEEAER   _ E _ _ _ E

12. CKUNEKL   _ _ U _ K _ _

13. EIALTDTU   L _ T _ _ _ _ _

14. ONMLE   _ _ _ _ N

15. ERETCJ   _ _ _ E _ T

16. TLRIE   _ _ _ E _

17. TPUEPP   _ _ P _ E _

18. IPEETLR   _ E _ _ _ _ E

19. DPRERCOUE   _ _ P R _ _ _ _ _

20. TPESMDAE   _ _ _ _ _ E _ E

Write sentences using words from above. Look up words when you are uncertain of their meanings.

_____

_____

_____

_____

_____

_____

_____

_____

_____

_____

_____

_____

_____

_____

Learn 1-3 New Words A Day

Name: _____

Date: _____

Please *unscramble* the words below.

PASTEL	DIMPLE	CONDUCTOR	CANVAS	COMMUNITY	BUREAU
BARBER	HEMISPHERE	ATTRACTION	ELEPHANT	CENTURY	CHORD
EXTEND	BYTES	EMERALD	DRAGON	CERTAIN	BOTHER
PREY	FINALLY				

1. ODHCR   _ H _ _ _

2. AGDONR   _ R _ _ _ N

3. ALYIFNL   _ _ _ _ _ L Y

4. OEHBTR   _ _ T _ _ R

5. AVNACS   C _ _ V _ _

6. OATRNTCTIA   _ _ _ R _ _ _ I O _

7. EMDAREL   _ M _ _ _ L _

8. MIDLPE   _ _ _ P L _

9. RABRBE   _ A _ B _ _

10. YMICNMUOT   _ O _ _ _ _ _ T _

11. ATICRNE   C E _ _ _ _ _

12. SEEHRPIHEM   H _ _ _ _ P _ _ R _

13. TDNEEX   _ _ _ _ N D

14. NTYUERC   C E _ _ _ _ _

15. TEYBS   _ Y _ _ _

16. HTEEPLNA   _ _ _ _ H A _ _

17. RUAEBU   _ _ R _ A _

18. CDROCUONT   _ O _ _ _ _ _ _ R

19. PELSAT   _ A _ _ E _

20. RPYE   P _ _ _

Write sentences using words from above. Look up words when you are uncertain of their meanings.

_____

_____

Learn 1-3 New Words A Day

Please *unscramble* the words below.

CENTIMETER	GOAL	CLAIM	ALLIGATOR	EQUATOR	IGLOO
BLOWN	GHOST	FINGER	AFFECTION	IMMIGRANT	DECADE
CROOKED	CHOIR	EXCEPT	FIFTY	FURNITURE	BOOMTOWN
GOOSE	FRAGILE				

1. MTRIETNECE   _ E _ T _ M _ _ _ _

2. YITFF   F _ _ _ _

3. NGFREI   _ I _ _ E _

4. ORDKCOE   _ R O _ _ _ _

5. RHICO   _ _ O _ _

6. OGIOL   _ _ _ _ O

7. LIEAFGR   _ _ _ _ I L _

8. TGIAINMRM   _ _ _ _ G _ _ _ T

9. GESOO   _ _ _ _ E

10. RFIRTEUUN   _ _ _ _ _ T U _ _

11. ECEDAD   D E _ _ _ _

12. OHSTG   _ _ _ _ T

13. CAIETNFFO   _ _ F _ _ _ _ O _

14. ALGO   _ _ _ L

15. ARLTAGLIO   _ L _ I _ _ _ _ _

16. ONMOOBWT   _ _ O _ _ O _ _

17. AMILC   _ _ _ I _

18. OBNLW   _ _ O _ _

19. ERUTQOA   _ _ U _ T _ _

20. EPTCXE   _ _ C E _ _

Write sentences using words from above. Look up words when you are uncertain of their meanings.

....

_____

Spelling Test

Your Answers		Correct Spelling If Incorrect	
1		1	
2		2	
3		3	
4		4	
5		5	
6		6	
7		7	
8		8	
9		9	
10		10	
11		11	
12		12	
13		13	
14		14	
15		15	
16		16	
17		17	
18		18	
19		19	
20		20	

Spelling Test

Your Answers	Correct Spelling If Incorrect
1	1
2	2
3	3
4	4
5	5
6	6
7	7
8	8
9	9
10	10
11	11
12	12
13	13
14	14
15	15
16	16
17	17
18	18
19	19
20	20

Spelling Test

Your Answers		Correct Spelling If Incorrect	
1		1	
2		2	
3		3	
4		4	
5		5	
6		6	
7		7	
8		8	
9		9	
10		10	
11		11	
12		12	
13		13	
14		14	
15		15	
16		16	
17		17	
18		18	
19		19	
20		20	

Spelling Test

Your Answers

1
2
3
4
5
6
7
8
9
10
11
12
13
14
15
16
17
18
19
20

Correct Spelling If Incorrect

1
2
3
4
5
6
7
8
9
10
11
12
13
14
15
16
17
18
19
20

Spelling Test

Your Answers	
1	
2	
3	
4	
5	
6	
7	
8	
9	
10	
11	
12	
13	
14	
15	
16	
17	
18	
19	
20	

Correct Spelling If Incorrect	
1	
2	
3	
4	
5	
6	
7	
8	
9	
10	
11	
12	
13	
14	
15	
16	
17	
18	
19	
20	

Spelling Test

Your Answers		Correct Spelling If Incorrect	
1		1	
2		2	
3		3	
4		4	
5		5	
6		6	
7		7	
8		8	
9		9	
10		10	
11		11	
12		12	
13		13	
14		14	
15		15	
16		16	
17		17	
18		18	
19		19	
20		20	

Spelling Test

Your Answers	Correct Spelling If Incorrect
1	1
2	2
3	3
4	4
5	5
6	6
7	7
8	8
9	9
10	10
11	11
12	12
13	13
14	14
15	15
16	16
17	17
18	18
19	19
20	20

Spelling Test

Your Answers

1
2
3
4
5
6
7
8
9
10
11
12
13
14
15
16
17
18
19
20

Correct Spelling If Incorrect

1
2
3
4
5
6
7
8
9
10
11
12
13
14
15
16
17
18
19
20

Spelling Test

Your Answers

1 _____
2 _____
3 _____
4 _____
5 _____
6 _____
7 _____
8 _____
9 _____
10 _____
11 _____
12 _____
13 _____
14 _____
15 _____
16 _____
17 _____
18 _____
19 _____
20

Correct Spelling If Incorrect

1 _____
2 _____
3 _____
4 _____
5 _____
6 _____
7 _____
8 _____
9 _____
10 _____
11 _____
12 _____
13 _____
14 _____
15 _____
16 _____
17 _____
18 _____
19 _____
20

Spelling Test

Your Answers	Correct Spelling If Incorrect
1	1
2	2
3	3
4	4
5	5
6	6
7	7
8	8
9	9
10	10
11	11
12	12
13	13
14	14
15	15
16	16
17	17
18	18
19	19
20	20

Spelling Test

Your Answers	Correct Spelling If Incorrect
1	1
2	2
3	3
4	4
5	5
6	6
7	7
8	8
9	9
10	10
11	11
12	12
13	13
14	14
15	15
16	16
17	17
18	18
19	19
20	20

Spelling Test

Your Answers	Correct Spelling If Incorrect
1	1
2	2
3	3
4	4
5	5
6	6
7	7
8	8
9	9
10	10
11	11
12	12
13	13
14	14
15	15
16	16
17	17
18	18
19	19
20	20

Spelling Test

Your Answers	Correct Spelling If Incorrect
1	1
2	2
3	3
4	4
5	5
6	6
7	7
8	8
9	9
10	10
11	11
12	12
13	13
14	14
15	15
16	16
17	17
18	18
19	19
20	20

Spelling Test

Your Answers

1
2
3
4
5
6
7
8
9
10
11
12
13
14
15
16
17
18
19
20

Correct Spelling If Incorrect

1
2
3
4
5
6
7
8
9
10
11
12
13
14
15
16
17
18
19
20

Class: _____

Day	Week:					Week:					Week:					Week:				
	M	T	W	Th	F	M	T	W	Th	F	M	T	W	Th	F	M	T	W	Th	F
Date																				
Assignments																				
1																				
2																				
3																				
4																				
5																				
6																				
7																				
8																				
9																				
10																				
11																				
12																				
13																				
14																				
15																				
16																				
17																				
18																				
19																				
20																				
21																				
22																				
23																				
24																				
25																				
26																				
27																				
28																				
29																				
30																				
31																				
32																				

Class: _____

		Week:					Week:					Week:					Week:				
Day		M	T	W	Th	F	M	T	W	Th	F	M	T	W	Th	F	M	T	W	Th	F
Date																					
Assignments																					
	1																				
	2																				
	3																				
	4																				
	5																				
	6																				
	7																				
	8																				
	9																				
	10																				
	11																				
	12																				
	13																				
	14																				
	15																				
	16																				
	17																				
	18																				
	19																				
	20																				
	21																				
	22																				
	23																				
	24																				
	25																				
	26																				
	27																				
	28																				
	29																				
	30																				
	31																				
	32																				

Week	Monday	Tuesday	Wednesday	Thursday	Friday
1					
2					
3					
4					
5					
6					
7					
8					
9					
10					
11					
12					
13					
14					
15					
16					
17					
18					

Notes

Made in the USA
Columbia, SC
20 September 2019